W9-CFC-153

PETE SAMPRAS

Great Athletes

PETE SAMPRAS

Calvin Craig Miller

**MORGAN
REYNOLDS**
Incorporated

Greensboro

PETE SAMPRAS

Copyright © 1998 by Calvin Craig Miller

Photos courtesy of

AP/Wide World Photos

Miller, Calvin Craig, 1954-.
  Pete Sampras / Calvin Craig Miller. —1st ed.
    p. cm. — (Great athletes)
  Includes bibliographical references and index.
  Summary: Follows the life and career of the professional tennis player who had won three
Wimbledon championships by the age of twenty-four.
  ISBN 1-883846-26-9
      1. Sampras, Pete—Juvenile literature. 2. Tennis players—United States—
Biography—Juvenile literature. [1. Sampras, Pete. 2. Tennis players] I. Title
II. Series.
GV994.S16M55 1998
796.342 ' 092—dc21
[b]

                                                                    97-48344
                                                                         CIP
                                                                          AC

Printed in the United States of America
First Edition

To Ruth

Contents

Chapter One 9

Chapter Two 15

Chapter Three 22

Chapter Four...27

Chapter Five 35

Chapter Six...40

Chapter Seven 45

Chapter Eight 50

Chapter Nine 56

Glossary 61

Bibliography 62

Index 63

Chapter One

When Pete Sampras first picked up an old wooden tennis racket he found stored in the basement of his family's home in Potomoc, Maryland he felt a power he had never experienced before. The racket seemed charged with wonder, like a magic wand. Soon, Pete's family became used to hearing the steady rhythm of Pete slamming tennis balls against the wall.

Pete worked steadily at improving his tennis game. Hard work came naturally to the entire Sampras family. His father, Soterios, called Sam, had grown up in Chicago, the son of Greek and Eastern European immigrants. He moved to Washington, D.C., in 1965, where he met Pete's mother, Georgia Vroustrous. Georgia had left her native country of Greece when she was 19, before she spoke English. She worked in a beauty parlor when she met Sam Sampras. Pete was born in Washington on August 12, 1971, the third of four children: Stella and Gus, both older than Pete, and his little sister, Marion.

Sam Sampras worked as an aerospace engineer for the government. Although he earned a good salary, he also worked nights at a Virginia delicatessen in which he was part owner. In 1978, Sam got a job offer from an aviation company in Rancho Palos Verdes, California. Sam and Georgia packed their four children, all their belongings and a parrot named Jose in their Ford Pinto and headed west. "We looked like the Griswalds," remembers Gus, referring to the series of Chevy Chase comedy movies.

Six-year-old Pete soon made a wonderful discovery about the family's new home in Rancho Palos Verdes. In the public parks of nearby Torrance, well-kept tennis courts gleamed in the California sunshine. Soon, Pete found other boys to spend hours on the court with him.

One day Pete's father finally came to watch him play. Sam considered tennis to be a sport for the idle rich. But as he watched his son streak across the court after the ball, he was astonished. "I had never seen anyone get on the court and hit the ball so smoothly," Sam later told a *Sports Illustrated* writer. "Like it was the easiest thing in the world."

Pete and older sister Stella, who also loved the sport, would have been satisfied to spend their lives on the courts. Sam and Georgia began going with them. They served balls to their children, at first hoping to save the expense of lessons. Soon, other people began watching the thin, tan boy who seemed able to make the ball and racket do whatever he willed.

One day, two men Sam had never met before took him aside. They convinced him that his son would waste a very great talent if he did not sign on with a professional coach.

The coach Sam chose was probably not who the two strangers had in mind. He approached Dr. Peter Fischer, a pediatrician and amateur player. They discussed the possibility of Fischer's coaching Pete. Fischer was willing and the talk turned to money.

"So how much do you charge?" Sam Sampras asked.

"Nothing," Fischer replied.

Pete Sampras has developed into one of the most powerful tennis players ever.

"You're hired," Sam said.

Later, Fischer's qualifications as a coach were questioned. But Fischer formed a strong bond with Pete. He quickly recognized Pete's talents and poured his energy into molding the boy into a champion.

Pete's focus on tennis meant he had to sacrifice activities his friends enjoyed, such as hanging out with friends. His best buddies were those he met at junior tournaments, some of whom would become professional tennis players themselves.

The gawky, dark-haired boy was a mystery to most of his classmates. They had no idea how strongly ambition burned inside him. Some thought he was shallow and boring. Even his coach found Pete introverted off the court. "He's quiet almost to the point of being dull," Fischer said.

Although Dr. Fischer remarked on how Pete concealed his feelings, he also encouraged this tendency. He drilled Pete on remaining emotionless on the court and on how to maintain composure even during the most intense competition. Occasionally, Pete threw his racket or cried in frustration. This always brought a strong warning from his coach.

Pete eventually mastered his stony "game face." It soon set his opponent's nerves on edge. No one knew what he was thinking on the other side of the net. But after he had learned how to bottle his feelings on court, it became more difficult to show them off the court. As he grew into adolescence, Pete became difficult to get to know. He went through his entire teenage years without a girlfriend.

All the while, Pete felt he was just a normal guy. He listened to rock and roll, becoming a great fan of the Eagles and Cat Stevens. He admired sports legends like Joe DiMaggio, and

Rod Laver was young Pete's model for the type of tennis player he wanted to be as a professional.

often took them as role models.

By far his most important role model became Rod Laver, an Australian tennis player whose career stretched from the 1950s through the 1970s. Laver could play well on any surface, from grass to clay, and cast a tall shadow over every other player of his day. During his career, he won all four of the major events called "the Grand Slam"—the U.S. Open, the Australian Open, the French Open and Wimbledon in Great Britain.

Fischer decided to take advantage of Pete's admiration of Laver's tennis style. He began bringing old 16-millimeter films of Laver's tournaments to the Sampras house. In the days before VCRs were common, the two would cut off the lights in one room and watch the flickering images of the Australian legend winning matches. Fischer often took his meals with the Sampras family. Pete developed a bad habit he has kept to this day. He wolfed his food down, anxious to get back to the film lessons.

Shy with most people, Pete would let his guard down and joke with his coach. "Did you save any lives today?" he would ask and flash the broad grin that soon earned him the nickname "Sweet Pete." The two would share a laugh, then Fischer would order Pete to hit one hundred forehand ground strokes down the line, followed by another one hundred cross court.

Spectators at Pete's practices often came away amazed. He was developing confidence in his game. He heard what adults said about how good a player he was becoming. He wanted to reach Laver's level of greatness, maybe higher.

Chapter Two

Dr. Peter Fischer became determined to make his young student a champion. The control Fischer demanded over Pete created strains in their relationship. Fischer was a brilliant man, with an IQ of 190. Although he had never taught tennis before, he wanted to shape Pete to his own vision. Fischer thought Pete might even change the way the game was played. Pete, who occasionally rebelled, later said it felt like Fischer wanted to put his brain in Pete's body. No one challenged Fischer's control, not even Pete's parents. Sam and Georgia did not want to become like so many overbearing "tennis parents," who hover about every minute during training and matches. So Fischer became almost a third parent to Pete, helping shape his character between the ages of nine and nineteen.

Fischer remade Pete's tennis strokes. When Pete was fourteen, Fischer insisted he stop hitting backhand shots with two hands. It was time to develop a one-handed backhand.

Pete was still at times, uncertain of his abilities. He was proud of his two-handed backhand, and frustrated by the order to change it. He knew other players had switched when they were having trouble with their two-handed shots. But why change when he was winning matches?

"My two-handed shot was not only a good shot, it was my *best* shot," Pete later told a writer for *Tennis Magazine*. "Abandoning my best shot was frustrating, controversial and risky."

The first time Pete tried the shot, the ball flew over the fence. Pete cried. Fischer refused to allow him to return to the two-handed style.

Pete's first tournament with the one-hander was at the Easter Bowl tournament in 1985. His ability to control the ball left him. His new shot seemed an ugly, cumbersome thing. He lost in the first round of the main draw, and immediately lost again in consolation.

Pete continued to lose matches as his ranking among junior players dropped rapidly. Losing matches wore on Pete's nerves and eroded his confidence. But Fischer insisted he stick with the new shot.

After a year of playing badly with the one-handed backhand, Pete rebelled. He went to his father and other coaches, and told them the new shot simply was not working. Even Robert Lansdorf, another coach who was helping Pete, agreed he should go back to the two-handed shot.

None of it convinced Fischer. Pete later recalled his coach's stubborn response.

"No," Fischer said. "You're sticking with the one-hander. Trust me. This is a move for the long run. It is a risky move, but it's the right one."

Pete reluctantly decided to tough it out a little longer with the one-hander. As he continued to lose matches, he began to get the feel of the shot. By the summer he turned sixteen, he had turned the corner. When, at the end of the summer, Pete beat Michael Chang, a highly regarded young player and future

Both Pete and Stella were coached free of charge by Dr. Peter Fischer.

professional great, at a U.S. Boy's tournament in Kalamazoo, Michigan, the shot that had been Pete's burden became his greatest strength.

"I accepted that it was a shot I was going to hit forever," Pete said. "The older and stronger I got, the better the shot became."

Fischer had other inventive coaching ideas. He did not want Pete to give away any clues about his shots before he hit them. He began calling out the serve he wanted Pete to hit after the ball was in the air. "You can't read Pete's serve, because his motion is the same for all his serves until he hits the ball," Fischer remembers. "I have him throw the ball up and then I'd call the serve—flat, topspin. He couldn't have a different motion because *he* didn't know what he was going to serve until I called it."

Fischer overmatched the still short and skinny boy, playing him in age classes for boys several years older. The strategy cost Pete some early disappointments, but also landed him in some prestigious tournaments early on. Pete met boys who would later mature into the tennis stars of the 1990s. He played Michael Chang, a player whose background was the opposite of Pete's in many ways. While Pete's parents kept their distance from his game, Chang's parents, both research chemists, monitored their son's tennis closely. Chang was a devout Christian and brought a work ethic to his game that matched Pete's.

It was at the camp for the 1987 U.S. Tennis Association Junior Davis Cup that he met another of his future professional rivals, Jim Courier. Courier was a driven competitor, but easygoing off court. Like Pete, he enjoyed baseball and rock-and-roll. He rooted for the Cincinnati Reds, listened to the rock group R.E.M., and played guitar and drums. Courier later said

Pete has competed against Michael Chang since his earliest years in tennis.

that while he wondered if he would make it to the ranks of world class tennis players, Pete seemed to know that he would.

Players at the Junior Davis Cup Camp started every morning with a 6:30 run. Pete often showed up groggy for the early morning run and was always the last to answer the call. He took some ribbing from the older players.

"He was the camp baby," Courier recalled later.

In 1988, at the age of 17, Pete took an even greater risk than switching tennis strokes. He dropped out of high school. He felt he had to take advantage of his skills by turning professional as soon as possible.

Pete remained almost unnoticed his first year as a pro. His greatest achievement was a semifinal berth in a tournament in Schenectady, New York. He did have one turn of good luck: an invitation to spend a week at the Connecticut home of Ivan Lendl. Lendl had won the U.S. Open tournament three times and was glad to offer advice to a young player with potential.

"The guy practically killed me," Pete said later. "Lendl had me biking twenty miles a day, talking to me about discipline and working hard and practicing until I couldn't walk home."

By the end of 1987, Pete had become one of the top hundred players in the world. He had reached the quarterfinals of several major tournaments and had teamed up with his old friend Jim Courier to win a doubles event in Rome.

But trouble developed as Pete began his climb into the professional ranks. Coach Fischer became dissatisfied. He had never been paid for his work. Now that Pete was earning money as a tennis player, Fischer thought that should change. One day he told Pete he was thinking about quitting. He wanted Pete to think it over for the next year.

Pete did not want to spend a year on the decision. He called Fischer the next day.

"Make your decision," Pete said. "It's now or never." Fischer refused to be pressured. The teacher and pupil parted company.

Not long afterward, Pete made it to the second round of the 1989 U.S. Open in New York City, defeating defending champion Mats Wilander in an upset. Although he did not win the tournament, the pleasure of his surprising victory over Wilander electrified him. "I just couldn't get over it," he said. "I remember driving back to the hotel around midnight, and I just couldn't believe I was still in the tournament. I mean, everyone expected me to lose."

Fans had seen a preview of greatness. Pete's second-round success in the 1989 U.S. Open was the first glimmer of the brilliant year that was to follow.

Chapter Three

Pete began 1990 ranked eighty-first in the world. It was a respectable position for a newcomer, but hardly high enough to attract attention as he made it to the fourth round of the year's first Grand Slam event, the Australian Open.

Changes had quietly taken place, however. Pete had grown from a short, skinny kid into a handsome, dark-haired young man who stood six feet tall. Many of the habits he forged as a boy endured. He remained tight-lipped about his feelings and opinions. He dressed conservatively and spent his money frugally, even as he began to earn more. He guarded his privacy.

In February, Pete passed another career milestone. He won his first title as a pro—a victory in the United States Pro Indoors tournament in Philadelphia. Then a hip injury sidelined him for the next two months. When he did return to competition, he soon won his second pro championship in Manchester, England. This was followed by the enormous letdown of being eliminated in the first round at Wimbledon.

Pete hated losing so quickly at the prestigious British tournament. He had set his sights on Wimbledon from the days he had watched his idol, Rod Laver, flickering across the screen at his California home. "It took a couple weeks to get over, because that was the tournament I was really gearing up to do well in," he said.

While Pete's fortunes rose and fell with each tournament, he was honing a powerful set of tennis skills. The one-handed backhand he had mastered at such great expense had given him a versatility far beyond the range of most young pros. Opponents could not predict his shots, because Dr. Peter Fischer had trained him to conceal them so well. And his serve had turned from a dart to a rocket, reaching speeds of more than 120 miles per hour.

Pete was still the best-kept secret in professional tennis. The tennis world expected little from Pete in the 1990 U.S. Open. He had just turned nineteen when he entered the tournament in September. The scene in Flushing Meadows, New York, offered much to dazzle a young man. Entertainment celebrities mingled with famed athletes like basketball legend Wilt Chamberlain and John Kennedy Jr. New York Mayor David Dinkins had air traffic rerouted from nearby LaGuardia Airport, so that an eerie quiet settled on the courts.

Pete's first opponent was his old mentor, Ivan Lendl, who had helped Pete train at his Connecticut home. Pete stunned his former host, sailing past Lendl in five sets. The victory set him up to face John McEnroe, a sentimental favorite with the crowd. The fiery tempered McEnroe had won four U.S. Open crowns, but had not made it past the second round in the two previous tournaments.

After losing, Lendl offered his own insights about how Pete could win the match. "It depends on how Sampras looks at that match," Lendl said. "If he breaks it down and looks at it as X or Y player, he's going to win. If he plays him as McEnroe, than he's going to lose."

Pete crushed McEnroe, 6-2, 6-4, 3-6, 6-3, which meant he won six games in the first set to McEnroe's two, six to McEnroe's four in the second set and so on. Pete only lost in the third set. Pete blasted seventeen aces (serves that could not be returned). McEnroe could only shake his head in bewilderment as the nineteen-year-old demolished his comeback hopes.

"He seems cool as a cucumber," McEnroe said, and admitted that he had let his own emotions run away with him at times during the match.

Now Pete was in the finals, facing Andre Agassi. The match could not have offered a more striking contrast of personalities and styles. Pete had played throughout with the quiet, seemingly emotionless attitude that he always brought to tournaments. His style seemed like a throwback to the 1960s, when players rarely showed their personalities on the court. Agassi was a bearded, brash young man who wore neon colors, in contrast to Pete's simple white uniform. He showed exuberance and anger, on court and while talking to reporters, while Pete kept his cool.

Some thought the U.S. Open was Agassi's to lose. He had taken apart defending champion Boris Becker, remaining calm while Becker grumbled about his own play. He had masterfully returned Becker's serve and had not missed a serve after the fifth game of the first set.

Pete's powerful shots stunned the crowd almost as much as they did Agassi. His scorching serves bewildered the flamboyant star. Pete blasted thirteen aces to build his tournament total to one hundred. Agassi at times seemed numbed, almost paralyzed, as Pete's shots rocketed past him.

Agassi fell in three sets: 6-4, 6-3, 6-2. At nineteen, Pete

The colorful Andre Agassi was usually the crowd's favorite when he was matched against Pete.

became the youngest U.S. Open champion in history. Agassi graciously conceded. "I came here looking forward to putting on a good show, but definitely the better man won," he said. "When you can hit a serve 120 on the line, there's not much you can do about it."

The upset dismayed Agassi supporters, delighted those who were not, and sent reporters scrambling for the phones. When President George Bush, himself a tennis player and fan, learned that three Americans had made it to the U.S. Open semifinals, he had time to call only one. He chose Agassi. Some thought the president had snubbed the winner. Pete was astonished that the president had made time to call any player in the Open. A reporter asked if the president's choice of Agassi over Sampras bothered him. "No, no, no," Pete insisted. "The phone was off the hook."

After demolishing Agassi, Pete walked off the stadium court with the crowd's cheers ringing in his ears. He called his parents in California. They often did not watch his matches because they could not stand the stress of watching Pete compete. They had gone to see a movie and to walk in a mall. They first learned of their son's triumph when televisions in a store window flashed the news.

"They were more stunned than anything," Pete said. "They said, 'Congratulations, you worked hard and you deserve it. Now enjoy the next couple of weeks and then get back to work.'"

Pete could not sleep a minute the night after the final. The next morning, he looked into the cameras of the three major networks on the morning television shows, and millions got their first look at the youngest U.S. Open champion in history.

Chapter Four

The moment Pete Sampras won the U.S. Open, the spotlight of world attention turned on him. He had sought this recognition all his life. Yet, at first it overwhelmed him. Before, Pete had been able to come and go from his Florida condominium freely. Now people recognized him wherever he went. Strangers asked for autographs and reporters requested interviews.

"I've gone from being recognized around the tennis world to being recognized by anyone around the world," Sampras said. "Your private life isn't private anymore."

Pete seemed to enjoy the limelight. In the weeks following his victory, he gave many nationally televised interviews. He appeared as a guest on *The Tonight Show* with host Johnny Carson. He even played doubles with President Bush.

Pete seemed to be dealing easily with the press attention. In fact, he was enjoying the "honeymoon" sometimes given to young sports stars. He did not know that he would soon have to learn the rules of dealing with the press. That part of the job did not come easily to a young man who had not finished high school.

Pete's personality did not always make for a good story. He was easy going off court, quick to flash his big smile. But he did not tell interesting stories about his life and his vocabulary seemed limited to people who made their living with words. Some reporters groaned as Pete repeatedly used words like "awesome" and "totally awesome" to describe his victories.

Pete tried to stay friendly with the other players on the tour. He frequently dined with a foe the night before a match. Occasionally he flew to a tournament on Andre Agassi's jet or gave a joint interview with Jim Courier, where the two chatted about their junior tennis days. Courier even gave Pete the nickname "The Sweet One."

But friendships only went so far with Pete. Even his sister Stella could not provide any answers about what went on in Pete's head. When a reporter asked her what motivated her brother Stella said, "I don't even know. He doesn't show a lot of emotion."

Pete's game continued to improve. In December, he played in the Grand Slam Cup, a tournament open to the top sixteen players in the world. In the final match, he sailed past Brad Gilbert in three sets. Despite his loss, Gilbert thought it an honor to have played Sampras. "He's taking the game to the year 2000 range," Gilbert said afterward. "I'd like to buy some stock in him. He is the guy of the future. He has ice water in his veins."

Gilbert saw something in Pete's on-court personality many opponents had missed. Pete kept his emotions as well-hidden as he did his choice of serves. Off-court, Pete looked like the boy next door, smiling, good-natured and amiable. On court, he looked more like a relentless, emotionless machine.

This ability to control his emotions on court proved to be one of the greatest strengths he had learned from his childhood coach, Dr. Peter Fischer, who had taught Pete to "depersonalize" his opponents.

Jim Courier, one of Pete's few friends off the court, gave him the nickname "The Sweet One."

Pete may have learned this lesson too well. When he met his childhood idol, Rod Laver, Pete showed no excitement at meeting a player he had put on a pedestal since childhood. Their conversation was short and stiff. Afterwards, Pete acted like it was no big deal. He continued to acknowledge Laver as a model, but he would not allow himself to be awed by any tennis player.

Otherwise, Pete was still the sweet-natured young man everyone remembered from his boyhood. After winning $2 million in the Grand Slam Cup, he gave $250,000 of it to research a cure for cerebral palsy, a disease that had killed two of his aunts. He stayed in close touch with his parents and his sister Stella, who had become a successful college player in her own right, winning a National Collegiate Athletic Association doubles championship her senior year. She said that when Pete called her after the U.S. Open win, he sounded as if he had done no more than win another junior title. "I think I was more excited than he was," Stella said. "You know Pete, he's just so calm and laid-back. He just said, 'Hey, Stella, How're ya doing?'"

Pete's single-minded focus during his childhood and teens had kept him from experiencing anything like a typical adolescence. He had seldom dated. Following his U.S. Open win, he began a relationship with his first girlfriend, Delaina Mulcahy. She was a law student at Stetson University in St. Petersburg, Florida. A few of the people around Pete had suspicions about Delaina's motives in becoming involved with Pete. This was due in part to the fact they did not meet until after his big victory, and partly because of their age difference. Pete was nineteen, Delaina twenty-six. But most people who knew them believed they were in love. Some even credited Delaina with helping him keep his focus.

That was becoming a more difficult task. Expectations had risen for Pete and now, when he stumbled, the public wondered why. He played poorly in the first months of 1991. He suffered shin splints, along with foot, ankle, and calf injuries. He chose not to play in the Australian Open. Pain forced him to quit in his next two tournaments. He lost in the second round of the French Open. He lost again at Wimbledon, the prestigious event that meant so much to his ambitions, again in the second round. His play dropped to a relatively mediocre record of sixteen wins in twenty-seven matches by the end of July.

The sports world began to wonder. Was Pete Sampras a true great of his time or just another flash in the pan?

He recovered and won some tournaments in the second half of the year. But Pete knew that the Grand Slams were everything. And the time for defense of his U.S. Open crown grew nearer. The pressure began to build as September approached.

"I've found out what Michael Chang meant when he said being the youngest champion of slam is like carrying a backpack full of bricks around for the next year," Pete told a reporter in August.

As the 1991 U.S. Open approached, Pete's body healed from the chronic leg injuries that had plagued him the early months of the year. He worked hard, rebuilding the strength he had lost because of injuries. But, as his body healed and he grew stronger, he continued to brood about his level of play.

He turned in a disappointing performance at the French Open tournament that year. Pete made his way to the second round, only to be clobbered by Thierry Champion, 6-3, 6-1, 6-1. Players compete on clay at the French tournament, and Pete has always admitted that clay is not the best surface for his powerful, attacking style.

At Flushing Meadows in September for the U.S. Open, many hoped to see a repeat of Pete's victory the year before. It was not to be. Pete made it only as far as the quarterfinals, where his old friend Jim Courier trounced Sampras in four sets. Stefan Edberg went on to beat Courier and win the tournament.

Losing the tournament was disappointing, but what Pete said afterward tarnished his reputation. At the age of twenty, Pete was still learning how to deal with a national press that was not always kind to athletes. When reporters asked Pete for a reaction on the defeat, he admitted to feeling some relief. He used the same terms he had used prior to the tournament, saying he felt that a "load of bricks" had dropped from his shoulders. Within hours, he faced the backlash from other players and the press.

"What? Don't tell me that!" raged player Jimmy Connors, when told of Pete's remarks. Connors, a former U.S. Open champion who had also been beaten by Courier, apparently thought Pete had halfheartedly defended his title."That is the biggest crock I've ever heard, being relieved," Connors continued. "I spent my whole life trying to win seven (Opens) in a row, or whatever possible. To be the U.S. Open champion is the greatest feeling you could have. And to try to do it again is what you live for. If these guys aren't living for that, something is wrong."

Pete's remarks also puzzled Jim Courier. Courier's response added to the public picture of Pete as a spoiled tennis brat. "Really, how much pressure does Pete have?" he said. "He'll never have to work another day in his life. He's got millions in the bank and he's twenty years old. I really think he should be able to swing freely and have fun with the game. Everybody

Pete did not perform well at the 1991 U.S. Open.

would trade places with him. He has the world at his feet. You should enjoy yourself in that situation. But each person is different in how they handle pressure."

In fact, the dread of a press backlash if he lost the tournament had contributed to Pete's pressure in the first place. He had never been as concerned about the money as how he would appear in the public spotlight. Now Pete was learning the hard way that public figures must weigh their words carefully.

"That really didn't come out right," Sampras said later about his "load of bricks" comments. "The perception was that I was glad I lost. I wasn't relieved I lost, but I said it and everybody was on my butt about it."

Nothing Pete said could change the first impression created by his statements. Unfortunately, these few words are still what most fans remember about his performance at the 1991 U.S. Open. Pete had been naive not to realize how his quoted remarks would play out of context. He tried to put his frustration aside, to look at the controversy as part of his growing process, as he battled for every title he could win after the 1991 Grand Slams ended. He earned some redemption for his U.S. Open loss and his media gaffe, when he turned in a brilliant performance to win the ATP World Championship in Frankfurt, Germany.

Pete turned in a more than respectable year in 1991 and entered the Davis Cup competition with a 36-6 record. And as Courier pointed out, Pete had already made a fortune.

But money was not what drove Pete Sampras. He still longed to take his place among the idols of his youth, the tennis champions of the 1960s and 1970s—to win more Grand Slam tournaments and learn how to deal with the press.

Chapter Five

Attitudes toward the Davis Cup competition are often different in America than in other parts of the world. Many Americans consider it to be just another tournament, not on the same level of importance as the Grand Slams. But in many other countries, the Davis Cup is the most critical event of the tennis year.

The tournament pits teams from individual countries against one another, somewhat in the manner of the Olympics. After a number of rounds, the teams from the two top nations play each other. The Davis Cup goes home with the victorious team.

In late 1991, Pete Sampras entered the competition with mixed feelings. He wanted to win, of course, as he does in any tournament. Yet the sting of his loss in the U.S. Open lingered. He was still focused on winning another Grand Slam event. He knew the Davis Cup was important, but it did not figure in his personal plan as highly as it did for many European athletes and fans.

The United States squad entered the competition as a heavy favorite. Pete also had a formidable record—36 wins, 6 losses. By the time the U.S. team reached the finals held in Lyons, France, the hosting French team was the underdog.

Pete faced a match that looked easy. Henri Leconte was a 31-year-old player who had undergone back surgery only four months before. Leconte did not seem a very threatening foe to a powerful player more than ten years his junior. But Leconte had once made himself an idol to the French crowds, with his attacking, flamboyant style and his many wins. He wanted a comeback.

Pete's American rival, Andre Agassi, knew firsthand, from his own style, how flamboyance combined with wins could excite crowds. He also knew how French crowds could charge a home court for their Davis Cup team. He considered himself better prepared for his Davis Cup match than Pete was. Agassi told reporters that he counted it good fortune that he would play ahead of Pete. "I'm comfortable with (Davis Cup play), because I know what to expect out there more than Pete," Agassi said. "I think there are a few more nerves involved when you play first. I've done it a few more times already. I think this can help us to get an early lead."

Agassi did win his match. Then Pete and Leconte took the court, with the burden of U.S. hopes shifting now to Sampras.

Leconte quickly nailed Sampras in straight sets, 6-4, 7-5, 6-4. He got his French fans into the match early, putting Sampras down and keeping him there. Leconte showed the colorful and fiery personality his crowds loved, pumping his fist in the air after each win, as the cries of "Henri, Henri" from 8,000 spectators echoed through the arena.

As defeat closed in, Pete showed one of the few physical clues he ever displays of losing his stride. His shoulders began to drop, his slump betraying his sense of frustration. The crowd, too, sensed the American nearing defeat. They cheered every

Henri Leconte had the support of the French fans at the 1991 Davis Cup competition held in Lyon, France.

error Pete made. When the match was finally over, Pete offered no excuse. "I just wasn't ready," he said.

In 1991, Pete had seemed unready almost every time the pressure mounted. How could he have played so well, earned such a great record, only to collapse when national spotlights focused the most attention? Despite the money and his current fame, Pete knew he could not continue to fold under pressure if he ever was to take his place in the record books beside his boyhood heroes.

It was beginning to look like Pete Sampras was a player who played well until he faced a great challenge. He was getting a reputation as someone who choked when the pressure was on.

Pete took one step to correct the problem as 1992 arrived. He decided it was time to have a coach again and hired Tim Gullickson. Tim was a knowledgeable ex-player who was easy to talk to, a tough-as-nails trainer, and an expert in spotting what made the difference between winning and losing under pressure. He and his twin-brother, Tom, had played the pro circuit together in the 1970s. Tim Gullickson had played with determination and skill during his professional career, but lacked the talent to become a star. He had found his true calling as a coach. He was soft-spoken but hard driving. Unlike Pete, he enjoyed gabbing with reporters. He went on so long during one interview that he looked up to find the writer had fallen asleep.

"Tim is always willing to talk," Pete said.

Luckily, Tim and Pete formed a quick bond. It looked like they might have a long road returning Pete to the level of player he wanted to be. Pete mounted a strong effort at the 1991 Wimbledon, the tournament he wanted most to win. He defeated defending champion Michael Stich and made it to the semifinals, but then lost to a hard-serving Goran Ivanisevic.

Pete went on to represent the United States in the 1992 Summer Olympics. Under the hot sun of Barcelona, Spain, Russian Andrei Cherkasov tortured Pete in a long five-set defeat. Pete then teamed up with Jim Courier for a doubles match, and the U.S. again suffered a defeat, this time at the hands of Spanish players Sergio Casal and Emilio Sanchez.

Next it was time for Pete to return to the scene of his greatest triumph and most embarrassing fiasco, the U.S. Open. Pete began the tournament with a brisk charge, hoping to get rid of the doubt that had plagued him the year before. He played top quality tennis through the semifinals, where he took apart top-seeded Jim Courier in three sets. It looked as if Pete might regain his U.S. Open crown and begin again his quest for the Grand Slam victories he had dreamed of as a boy.

Then bad luck struck. Soon after his match with Courier, Pete was seized with intestinal cramps. Diarrhea and dehydration continued through the next day. Doctors stuck needles in his arms and gave him intravenous fluids, but the pain and nausea lingered. Defending U.S. Open champion Stefan Edberg took advantage of his opponent's weakness to take a four-set victory over Pete.

"My head was dropping and (Edberg) saw that," Sampras said afterward. "I just felt it slipping away."

Both Pete and his new coach, Tim Gullickson, hoped that Pete was not slipping away for good. The history of tennis is littered with would-be greats who only enjoyed their moment in the sun at one or two Grand Slams. As 1992 neared its end, Pete and his supporters had to wonder if he would become one more footnote in Grand Slam history.

Chapter Six

The U.S. Open defeat ended Pete's chances for a Grand Slam win in 1992. But momentum began to shift his way as the year drew to a close. During the Davis Cup, where he had played poorly the year before, Pete teamed with John McEnroe to defeat Henri Leconte and his partner. The victory went a long way toward erasing the sting of his earlier defeat in Lyons, France. "It's the best two sets of doubles I've ever played," Pete said. "You can't replace this feeling."

Pete continued to gain confidence through the spring, winning four championships by the end of April. He reached the semifinals of the Australian Open and helped the United States win the World Team Cup. The French Open dealt Pete another frustration, as he fell to eventual champion Sergi Bruguera. Even so, his performance in other tournaments was enough to land Pete the top seed going into Wimbledon.

Pete had to endure some pain to play through the early matches at the prestigious British tournament. On the Wednesday before the tournament began, tendinitis in his right shoulder hurt so badly he could not brush his teeth. He winced during matches and his nose bled during his third round victory over Byron Black of Zimbabwe. He considered withdrawing at one point. But he was too determined to quit. Wimbledon was too large a prize to give up on.

The British sports press and fans had a clear favorite among the Americans—and it was not Pete. Their favorite was the colorful, outspoken and brash Andre Agassi. They saw Pete's conservative style, on the court and off, as a sign he had no personality. British newspapers even ran snide stories about him before he reached the semifinals. Pete would open a paper to read "PETE'S A BORE" in huge letters at the top of the page. One radio station took a survey, asking the question, "Whom would you most like to share strawberries and cream with at Wimbledon?" Out of 1,000 responses, Pete got one vote. When told about the results, he tried to shrug it off. "I let my racket do the talking," he said.

Although Pete tried to remain nonchalant, the hostility began to wear on him. Taught to keep his on-court cool—one of the reasons the British thought him boring—he began to lose his temper under the pressure. When he defeated the last British player in the fourth round, he even swore at the crowd and raised his clenched fist.

The crowd's antagonism increased. Agassi fans hoped their flamboyant favorite would end Sampras' run in the semifinals. Agassi's fans included the actress and singer Barbra Streisand, who applauded every time Pete made an error. Streisand did not have many opportunities to clap that day. Pete downed Agassi, 6-2, 6-2, 3-6, 3-6, 6-4. He went on to defeat Boris Becker in the semifinals and his old nemesis, Jim Courier, in the finals. American Pete Sampras won the tournament crown on July 4.

Pete had earned his second Grand Slam title, finally shaking the curse that had dogged him since he attempted to defend his

U.S. Open title in 1991. But the reception he got after his victory was far from gracious.

"How does it feel to be the most hated man at Wimbledon?" a British reporter asked after the final match. One newspaper ran the results under a stars-and-stripes design headline that read "BORED ON THE FOURTH OF JULY."

Some writers rallied to Pete's defense. John Feinstein of *Tennis Magazine* wrote that the crowds had cheered champions who had fits of bad temper and ill manners, such as John McEnroe and Jimmy Connors. These players shouted obscenities, baited umpires and threw rackets. When the same fans were treated to a performance by a world-class player whose worst sin was to refrain from such behavior, they called him a bore. Feinstein insisted Sampras was a better man than many of his flashier predecessors. "Sampras is exactly the kind of young man you would want your son to grow up to be," Feinstein wrote.

Pete went through a slump for several tournaments following Wimbledon. His new coach helped him through, keeping his spirits up and his training regimen disciplined even after the defeats.

Gullickson insisted that Pete work on yet another skill which might fit the "boring" label—the patience to take long, hard matches in stride. Gullickson's optimism and determination helped Pete maintain his own will to win. Gullickson soon became more than a good coach. He was one of Pete's closest friends.

As Pete prepared for the 1993 U.S. Open, a writer watched Pete train and saw an aspect of his personality that few had seen before. During his strenuous practice, Pete screamed, com-

Coach Tim Gullickson helped put Pete's game back on track.

plained, shouted, and laughed with joy. After making an ace, Pete shouted "Ice water in my veins!" Clearly, the emotionless mask Pete wore on court was part of his strategy.

Pete arrived at Flushing Meadows, in September with a renewed desire to retake the tournament that had first drawn him national and international attention. This time, Pete was no longer an unseasoned defender who could be undone by pressure. He felt if he could take the abuse he had gone through at Wimbledon, he could deal with whatever the U.S. Open could dish out.

He marched easily through the first four rounds of the U.S. Open, destroying his opponents with relative ease. He met a tough challenge in the quarterfinals, when he faced Michael

Chang, one of his old rivals from the junior tennis circuit. Pete always considered Chang to be "a pain" to play. He dropped the first set, but rallied in the second for a close victory, then exploded in the last two to bury Chang, 6-1, 6-1.

After the match, reporters asked Chang what he could have done to change the outcome. "There's really nothing you can do," he said. "When he's playing his best, he's practically unbeatable."

Pete's next two opponents soon agreed with Chang. He demolished Alexander Volkov to win the semifinals, and did the same to Cedric Pioline to earn the 1993 U.S. Open crown.

It was a sweet redemption for his embarrassing 1991 defeat. Besides that, it was another career milestone. Pete had won two Grand Slams in one year. After a two-year drought in the four greatest tournaments in tennis, Pete was back on the track to become one of the best tennis players ever.

Chapter Seven

Pete's 1993 back-to-back triumphs at Wimbledon and the U.S. Open, renewed interest in this twenty-two-year-old. He soon became the subject of much speculation. Could he continue his Grand Slam streak? The next test was the Australian Open, held in January 1994, where he had lost to Stefan Edberg in the semifinals the year before.

Pete sailed easily through the first round past Josh Eagle, and weathered a test in the second from a Russian nineteen-year-old named Yevgeny Kafelnikov. Kafelnikov kept Pete on the move, placing his shots brilliantly until Sampras finally struggled to earn an exhausting victory, 6-3, 2-6, 6-3, 1-6, 9-7.

From then on, winning came easier, all the way through his victory over Jim Courier in the semifinals. The win over Courier set up a final match with Todd Martin. Martin played much like Sampras, conservative, slow to anger, and hard to read on court.

As he had at times before, Pete met his opponent in a friendly setting before the match. They had dinner together the night before the finals. Facing a major world contest and an international spotlight in less than twenty-four hours, the two joked together over plates of pasta.

Pete served Martin less pleasant fare the next day, when he

beat him 7-6, 6-4, 6-4. The victory brought Pete another step closer to his goal of becoming the first man since his hero, Rod Laver, in 1965 to have consecutive wins at Wimbledon, the U.S. Open, and the Australian Open.

After the match, reporters asked Pete about the similarity between himself and the man he had just beaten. "It makes it more fun for me when people appreciate two guys who just go out and play tennis," Sampras said. "I think that's the way tennis should be played—with class, without losing your temper or embarrassing yourself."

If Sampras could win the French Open, he would have a chance to win all four Grand Slams consecutively. Perhaps the harshest opponent Pete faced in France would be the clay surface. Coach Tim Gullickson had tried to help him prepare by drilling him on clay in practice. Pete knew he would have to play the tournament of his life to win in France.

But it was not to be. Pete made it through four rounds, to the semifinals, where he faced his long-time buddy and rival, Jim Courier. Courier ousted Pete, 6-4, 5-7, 6-4, 6-4. The defeat snapped Pete's record of 27 consecutive match wins and put off his quest to match Laver's record for at least another year.

He rebounded quickly from the letdown. He returned to Wimbledon, where he been an unpopular champion the year before, confident and ready to compete.

If he had been good in his previous Wimbledon victory, Sampras' performance in the 1994 tournament was nothing short of uncanny. He dropped only one set and lost his serve only three times in the entire tournament. He fired serves like missiles at his opponents and placed drop volleys into the forecourt that stunned his foes. Every time the pressure rose,

so did the level of Pete's play. In the semifinals, he downed Todd Martin, who had beaten him the week before in a finals match at the Queens Club tournament.

In the Wimbledon finals, Pete faced Croatian player Goran Ivanisevic. Ivanisevic had played Pete well before, and held a 5-3 advantage going into the Wimbledon finals. He had fired 140 aces to that point and spent much of the week telling the press that he had reached a new level of power at Wimbledon. The two sparred in a war of words going into the match.

"Pete doesn't like to play me," Ivanisevic told reporters. The left-handed Ivanisevic added that Pete always struggled against his "lefty serves."

Pete found help against a left-handed foe. His coach's twin brother and former pro, Tom Gullickson, was also left-handed. He fired his best shots at Pete to ready him for the challenge against Ivansevic and later Pete proved himself up to the challenge. "There's no need to push a guy who pushes himself," Gullickson said. Everyone on Pete's side, including Pete, believed he had the power and momentum to win.

"I feel if I play my best or play well, I'm pretty tough to beat," Pete said. "I think I do everything well. I return well, serve well."

Sampras backed up his self-assessment in the finals. He wore Ivanisevic down by the third set, then cracked the Croatian in six straight games for the crown. Pete let loose the joy he felt, throwing his racquet and two shirts into the crowd.

Ivanisevic sat dazed in his chair, still shaken by the fury of Pete's onslaught. "Too good," was all Ivanisevic said.

Tim Gullickson boasted to the press that Pete had reached a point where every player had to respect him and few could stop him. "He is the perfect combination of raw power and great

Pete wore down the determined left-hander Goran Ivanisevic to win the 1994 Wimbledon crown.

touch," Gullickson said. "He knows that any tournament he enters is his to win."

Pete's momentum slowed during the final months of 1994. He took some time off after his Wimbledon victory to recover from a reoccurrence of tendinitis. He played in two Davis Cup matches in the Netherlands, but otherwise sat out the tour until the U.S. Open in late August.

Sampras entered the U.S. Open in less than his best form. It showed early on. He managed to hang on through three rounds, but his absence from tournament play had cost him the seemingly unstoppable power he had shown early in the year. He fell to an unseeded opponent, Jaime Yzaga of Peru. During the grueling three-and-a-half-hour match, pain shot through his back and a blister developed on a foot. Yzaga turned the tables on the player who had sent his foes racing over the courts of Wimbledon. Seeing that Sampras was having trouble moving, Yzaga fired groundstrokes mercilessly across the court and took a hard-earned victory in five sets.

Sampras finished the year on a disappointing note. He followed the U.S. Open defeat with a poor showing in the Davis Cup in Sweden. He dropped out of Davis Cup competition in the finals against Stefan Edberg, when the pain of a severe right hamstring proved too severe.

Despite his disappointing finish to the year, Pete had built such a commanding lead early on that he held onto his number-one ranking throughout the fall. He was learning to take his wins and losses in stride. Now, patience served him as well as talent. Yet, there was one new and terrifying loss that Pete had never experienced before. It would begin not with a loss on the tennis court, but a fall in a hotel room in Stockholm, Sweden.

Chapter Eight

While Pete struggled with his injuries and Stefan Edberg on the Davis Cup courts in Sweden, his coach, Tim Gullickson, endured a far worse ordeal.

It began with a fall in their Stockholm hotel. Gullickson was walking across the room when his legs suddenly gave way from under him. He crashed face-first through a glass table, ripping bloody scars down his face. Bleeding badly, Gullickson tried to telephone another coach on Pete's team. But the man could not understand what Gullickson was saying.

This occurred in October of 1994 and, upon their return home, doctors examined Coach Gullickson. Their first diagnoses were that Gullickson had suffered a heart attack or stroke. But the symptoms did not quite match either condition. Several months later, Gullickson was talking to his wife on the phone when his speech again became garbled. The Gullickson family pressed the doctors for more tests.

As Pete prepared for the Australian Open, it became clear that Tim Gullickson's health was worse than anyone had thought. Pete and Tim were running one day when Tim felt his strength leave him. He could run no more. He stopped, then passed out. He was rushed to a hospital in Melbourne, Australia.

This time the physicians finally delivered an accurate and terrible diagnosis: Gullickson had cancer of the brain. It was treatable, but his chances of survival did not look good.

At twenty-four, Pete had never witnessed a close friend having to struggle with a life-threatening disease. He carried the knowledge of Tim's illness as he walked onto the courts of the Australian Open to defend the title he had won the year before.

He opened up playing well through four rounds. Fans could tell no difference in the emotionless mask Pete wore on the court. The intimidating game face that told no foe of his intentions and caused so many to label him boring now became his defense against showing the public his private pain.

Pete did not crack until the semifinal round against Jim Courier. It happened during a changeover just after the start of the first set. Pete reached for a towel, then suddenly buried his face in it and wept. After regaining his composure, he splashed his face quickly with water, then went back onto the court.

Courier kept up the pressure on Sampras, shifting momentum his way. Then something cracked inside Pete. He grew nearly immobile and defenseless. Tears streamed down his face.

Pete's girlfriend, Delaina Mulcahy, called out "Come on, honey, get in there."

Courier looked puzzled. "Are you all right, Pete?" he shouted. "You know, we can do this tomorrow if you want."

His long-time rival and friend meant the words only as a gesture of sportsmanship. Courier had known Pete since his teens and had never seen him act this way. But it sounded like a taunt to Pete. Do this tomorrow? No one did that in Grand Slam tournaments. Pete took the court again in a rage, fired his twentieth ace of the match, and launched three more across the net until Courier began to break. Cramps seized Courier in the seventh game and he fell at last.

Pete had wanted nothing more than to get this round over with. With the victory in hand, he stalked back to the face the reporters.

Sports journalists abide by a long-standing tradition. No one roots for an athlete or a team. There are no cheers in press rooms. But as Pete had cracked, so did the press tradition. When Pete entered, reporters stood and applauded.

Not surprisingly, considering the emotional pain he was feeling, Pete did not hold on to keep his Australian Open crown. He did beat the staunch and well-disciplined Michael Chang in the semifinals, but lost to Andre Agassi in the finals. He would lose again that year in the French Open, the tournament that had dealt him nothing but defeat.

Pete pondered his losses and his public show of emotion as he flew back to his adopted hometown of Tampa, Florida. He did not like the fact that it took his tears to prove what his words and game could not—that he was human underneath the cold mask he wore to misdirect his on-court foes. At home, he dropped his luggage as if the weight of the world was his alone.

"I had just lost in the French and I came back home to Tampa, walked in the door and dropped my bags down—and just felt so depressed," he said. "That was the first time in my life I could ever remember feeling like that. I was down. The year wasn't going well."

Gullickson kept coaching Pete as he prepared to defend his Wimbledon crown. But instead of the daily workouts, Gullickson coached his star player by phone, three or four times a week.

The tournament where Pete had encountered his worst

A broken hearted Pete Sampras served as a pallberer at his beloved Coach Gullickson's funeral.

criticism, even in victory, provided exactly the lift he and Gullickson had hoped for. Pete fired 106 aces and won 124 of 132 service games at Wimbledon. He weathered four rounds and the semifinals, only to meet his outspoken opponent from the year before, Goran Ivanisevic in the semifinals. He battled Ivanisevic down to the wire, firing twenty-one aces to his foes's thirty-eight, but holding on to beat him by a single point in five sets.

He encountered Boris Becker in the finals. Becker had been a crowd pleaser that year, but he could not stand off Sampras. Pete fired twenty-three aces to Becker's sixteen and took a four-set triumph without facing a break point.

Ironically, Pete began to close in on his childhood heroes and tennis history as Gullickson's health declined. When Sampras took the court for any tournament in the world, foes knew he was the one to beat. He proved as much by seizing the second of his Grand Slam chances at the 1995 U.S. Open. He blasted his way through the first two rounds, survived a close call in the third, won two more in straight sets, then faced Courier in the semifinals. He took Courier down in four tough sets. Pete would meet one of his oldest rivals, the colorful Andre Agassi, in the final. Sampras won in the third set with seventy-six-mile-per-hour shot slicing away from Agassi.

Pete had done just what both he and his coach demanded. But his winning streak was not over. He had yet another day of glory at the Davis Cup. He teamed with Todd Martin for a doubles victory, that helped the United States defeat Russia and bring the trophy home to the U.S.

During the Davis Cup play, Pete kept a tight focus on his game and paid little attention to his surroundings. When asked about playing in Moscow Pete answered, "Outside of one trip to Red Square and a look at Lenin's tomb, my whole time here has been either in the hotel with room service or at the court."

On the heels of his triumph in Russia, Pete received the long dreaded news. On May 3, 1996, Coach Gullickson's cancer finally claimed him. Pete's beloved coach was dead.

Pete tried to give an eulogy at the funeral. He could not finish it. He carried Tim's casket as a pallbearer, a role he felt little prepared for. He had never been to a funeral in his life.

Athletes frequently dedicate their next victory to a lost peer or coach. The chance to do so eluded Pete for the first months of 1996. He lost at the Australian and French opens, and lost his Wimbledon crown as well.

He got his chance at the next U.S. Open. He worked his way methodically through the first four rounds, then played an exhausting match against Alex Corretja. Corretja kept Pete on the court for seven sets, even managing to keep his cool while running Sampras so hard that Pete vomited at one point. But Pete hung on for the win. In the semifinals, he outplayed Goran Ivanisevic, then pounded down Michael Chang in the final, 6-1, 6-4, 7-6 (7-3).

His girlfriend urged him to leave the past behind with his dedication of the tournament to Tim Gullickson. Tim had done his work well and so had Pete. Pete said his goodbye to the man who had helped the most in his adult career.

"I still felt his spirit and even though he's not here with us he's still very much in my heart," Pete said.

Chapter Nine

The Pete Sampras who dedicated his 1996 U.S. Open victory to his late coach was a much different man than he had been after winning his first Grand Slam. He had learned how to face a hard nosed press corp, how to win a major tournament even when he was not at his best, and how to triumph whether the crowd was with him or not. Now he had learned that he could win even when personal tragedy struck.

After Gullickson's death, Pete continued to dominate on the tennis court. At the 1997 Australian Open, he turned out a performance as hot as the blistering 100-degree heat to beat Carlos Moya in straight sets. He served 12 aces to Moya's two, and placed the ball with uncanny accuracy.

Pete later called it the toughest major he had won. He iced down an aching right arm after every match and practice. Against Moya, he busted racket strings after the second game of the match, the fourth, two more in the second set and another in the third. Throughout the grueling match, each man received support from his fans. Many of Pete's backers came from the large Greek community around Melbourne, who had adopted him as their own because of his Greek ancestry. The 20-year-old Moya was a crowd favorite for some because the young

Spaniard, who had entered the tournament unseeded, was an underdog. Moya also had movie star good looks, with long hair framing a handsome face.

But it was clear from the outset that it was not to be Moya's day. A reporter asked what he had learned from the match. Moya smiled. "Who's number one," he said.

Pete told the press that the most important part of the victory was that he was beginning 1997 with a win in one of the four tournaments he always targeted. "It's how you base your career, on Grand Slam titles," he said. "To have won one is a great start to the year."

The French Open, however, once again stopped Pete's momentum, and his quest for Laver's mark of four straight. The 1997 event proved a disaster for all the American players. Each was defeated before the finals, the first time they had been shut out since 1969. The French tournament remains the only Grand Slam where Pete has yet to earn a victory.

Pete arrived at Wimbledon in June eager to shake off the French Open loss. At the ceremonial opening of the new Court No. 1, he joined a group of players who had earned at least three Wimbledon victories: Boris Becker, Louise Brough, Margaret Court, Chris Evert, Billie Jean King, Rod Laver, John McEnroe, Martina Navratilova and John Newcombe. During the ceremony, he seemed ill at ease, digging at the grass with his toe. After the other players were summoned to receive commemorative plates, Pete was left standing alone until his name was called.

"I was the last one . . . and it hit me," Pete said. "For a second it felt like, What am I doing here?" The answer came in Pete's mind an instant after the question: He had joined the ranks of the greatest in the game. What feeling could be better?

He would soon know.

Rumors of Boris Becker's retirement had circulated for months prior to the tournament. But before he quit, Becker was determined to face Sampras at Wimbledon. He got his wish in the quarterfinals. It was not a pleasant experience for Becker. Pete took him apart, 6-1, 7-6, 6-1, 6-4. When the match ended, Becker met Pete at the net. He told his rival that this was his last Wimbledon. Pete had stolen the fire from Becker at this most prestigious of tournaments. In three prior matches there, Becker had never once broken Pete's serve. Even so, he told Pete it had been a pleasure to play him.

The next of Pete's victims said nearly the same thing. Todd Woodbridge—a fierce and determined player who had beat him the first time Pete played the tournament—took a pounding from Sampras. Afterward, he said he was honored. "It's something I'll talk about when I'm finished, how good he was," Woodbridge said.

The "honor" was short for Pete's final opponent, Frenchman Cedric Pioline. Pete took only 94 minutes to polish off Pioline, smoothly rolling to the title with a 6-4, 6-2, 6-4 victory.

After his historic fourth Wimbledon victory, Pete raised his arms and thumped his chest, with a smile for his new girlfriend, actress Kimberley Williams. No one had known much about Delaina and Pete's private life. Typically, Pete offered no explanation of what had broken them up. All the spectators knew was that Pete had a new girlfriend.

After this Wimbledon victory, the praise in tennis circles shifted to a new level. Speculation now was about his place in tennis history. He has yet to win four straight Grand Slams, as did his idol Rod Laver. But with ten Grand Slam titles, he moved

Pete's newest girlfriend is movie and stage actress Kimberley Williams.

closer to the top of the all-time great tennis players' list. Australian Roy Emerson still holds the record with twelve Grand Slam titles; Bjorn Borg and Rod Laver had eleven each. His current record matches that of the legendary Bill Tilden, the greatest American player of the 1920s. Moreover, some writers question whether comparisons with players of earlier eras are accurate, since more great players play now than at any time in history and the competition is much more fierce.

Pete said all he needs to say about his own chances after winning Wimbledon in 1997.

"I really have no fear," he said.

Pete Sampras towers over all his current rivals on the tour. One of them may beat him in a given tournament, but no one can match his overall performance. After losing his final match to him, Becker gave Pete the strongest praise one player can give another. "He has the power, he has the speed, he has the touch," Becker said. "He is the best player ever."

Pete gave Becker credit as well, for the good grace with which the German player stepped down. He said he hoped he could match Becker's class when he reached his own retirement. But he quickly added an important point.

"I am nowhere near that day," he said.

GLOSSARY

Ace: A serve hit so well that it is unreturnable.

Backhand: A stroke that forces the player to extend the racket hand across the body.

Doubles: A game played by four contestants, two to a side.

Forehand: A stroke used to return balls met on the racket-hand side of the body.

Forecourt: The area extending from the net to the service line.

Game: A single contest in a set, in which the winner makes four points, or two consecutive points after a deuce.

Match: A period of competition consisting of sets or groups of games. It may consist of two wins in three sets, or three of five.

Match point: A potentially game-winning point that, if successful, wins the match as well.

Seed: A system of ranking players at a tournament, so the top players have a greater chance of meeting in the finals.

Serve: Beginning the game by hitting the ball across the net to the opponent's side. The server hits the ball from behind the baseline into the opposite service court of the other player.

Set: The part of the match in which one player has won at least six games and leads by two games, or has won the tie break.

Set point: A potentially game-winning point that, if successful, will also win the set.

Straight set: A match won without the loss of a single set.

Tie breaker: 12-point scoring system used to determine a set winner when the score reaches six games all.

Umpire: The official who enforces the rules in a match.

Volley: To hit the ball before it strikes the court.

BIBLIOGRAPHY

Sports Illustrated, Sept 17, 1990, "Upset Time," Alexander Wolff.

The Sporting News, Sept. 17, 1990, "Sampras, a Cool 19, Aces the Open," Jim Martz.

People Weekly, Sept. 24, 1990, "Float Like a Butterfly, Serve Like a Bazooka," Andrew Abrahams, Cindy Dampier, Tom Cunneff.

Sports Illustrated, Oct. 22, 1990, "Focused," Bruce Newman.

Sports Illustrated, Sept. 16, 1991, "Open and Shut," Curry Kirkpatrick.

Tennis, January 1992, "Victorious Sampras Rides Hot Streak in 1992," Richard Finn.

Sports Illustrated, July 12, 1993, "Rockets on the 4th," Sally Jenkins.

Tennis, September 1993, "The Sweet One," David Higdon.

The Sporting News, Sept. 20, 1993, "From Start to Finish, It Was a Name-Tag Open," Tony Kornheiser.

Tennis, November 1993, "Bores are Better than Boors," John Feinstein.

Tennis, February 1994, "Player of the Year: Pete Sampras," Donna Doherty.

Tennis, July 1994, "Courier and Sampras Face Off," David Higdon.

Sports Illustrated for Kids, August 1994, "Pete Sampras: Tennis Player," David Higdon.

Tennis, September 1994, "Hail and Farewell," Mark Preston.

Sports Illustrated, June 12, 1995, "For Pete's Sake," staff.

Newsweek, July 3, 1995, "Different Strokes," Curry Kirkpatrick.

Tennis, August 1995, "Why I Abandoned My Best Shot," Pete Sampras.

The New York Times Magazine, Aug. 27, 1995, "Sampras or Agassi: A 90s Kind of Rivalry," Peter De Jonge.

Sampras: A Legend in the Works, H.A. Branham, Bonus Books, Inc., Chicago, 1996.

Tennis, February 1996, "Sampras' Heroics Secure Davis Cup," Christopher Clarey.

People Weekly, July 8, 1996, "Lesson of the Heart," staff.

Tennis, January 1997, "The Man Who Saved Tennis From Itself," Peter Bodo.

The New York Times, Jan. 20, 1997, "Sampras Beats Young Upstart in Hot 5-Setter," Robin Finn.

Web Pages

Slam Tennis (Web page), "Sampras Captures Australian Open Title," http://www.cmtcanada.com/SlamTennisAustralianOpen/jan26_aussie.

Tennis Magazine Online (Web page), "Sampras' Serve Wins Him 10th Grand Slam Title," Sandra Harwitt, http://www.tennis.com/slams/wdon97/final.htm

Index

1992 Olympics, 39
Agassi, Andre, 24-26, 36, 41, 52, 54
ATP World Championship, 34
Australian Open, 14, 22, 31, 40, 45-46, 50-52, 55-57

Becker, Boris, 24, 41, 54, 57-58, 60
Black, Byron, 40
Borg, Bjorn, 60
Brough, Louise, 57
Bruguera, Sergi, 40
Bush, President George, 26-27

Carson, Johnny, 27
Casal, Sergio, 39
Chamberlain, Wilt, 23
Champion, Thierry, 31
Chang, Michael, 16, 18-19, 43-44, 52, 55
Cherkasov, Andrei, 39
Cincinnati Reds, 18
Connors, Jimmy, 32-33, 42
Corretja, Alex, 55
Courier, Jim, 18, 20, 28-29, 32, 34, 39, 41, 45-46, 51-52, 54
Court, Margaret, 57

Davis Cup, 34-36, 49, 54
DiMaggio, Joe, 12

Dinkins, David, 23

Eagles, The, 12
Edberg, Stefan, 32, 39, 45, 49, 50
Emerson, Roy, 60
Evert, Chris, 57

Feinstein, John, 42
Fischer, Dr. Peter, 10, 12, 14-18, 20-21, 23, 28
French Open, 14, 31, 40, 46, 52, 55, 57

Gilbert, Brad, 28
Gullickson, Tim, 38-39, 42-43, 46-47, 49-56
Gullickson, Tom, 47, 55

Ivanisevic, Goran, 39, 47-48, 54-55

Kafelnikov, Yevgeny, 45
Kennedy Jr, John, 23
King, Billie Jean, 57

Lansdorf, Robert, 16
Laver, Rod, 13-14, 22, 30, 46, 57-58, 60
Leconte, Henri, 36-37, 40
Lendl, Ivan, 20, 23

Martin, Todd, 45-46, 54
McEnroe, John, 23-24, 40, 42, 57
Moya, Carlos, 56-57
Mulcahy, Delaina, 30, 51, 58
Navratilova, Martina, 57
Newcombe, John, 57

Pioline, Cedric, 44, 58

Sampras, Georgia Vroustrous, 9-10, 15
Sampras, Gus, 9
Sampras, Marion, 9
Sampras, Pete,
    birth, 9
    charitable contributions, 30
    childhood, 9-21
    death of coach, 55
    emotional reserve, 27-29, 50-52
    loses 1991 U.S. Open, 31-32
    press attention, 26-28, 31-32, 34, 41-42, 45, 52
    social life, 30, 58-59
    training, 10, 12, 14-16, 18-21, 38
    wins 1990 U.S. Open, 23-26
    wins 1991 ATP World Championship, 34
    wins 1992 Wimbledon, 40-41
    wins 1993 U.S. Open, 43-44
    wins 1994 Australian Open, 45-46
    wins 1994 Wimbledon, 46-47
    wins 1995 U.S. Open
    wins 1995 Wimbledon, 53-54
    wins 1996 U.S. Open, 55
    wins 1997 Australian Open, 56-57
    wins 1997 Wimbledon, 57-58
    wins first pro title, 22
Sampras, Soterios (Sam), 9-12, 15
Sampras, Stella, 9-11, 17, 28, 30
Sanchez, Emilio, 39
Sports Illustrated, 10
Stetson University, 30
Stevens, Cat, 12
Stitch, Michael, 38
Streisand, Barbra, 41

Tennis Magazine, 16, 42
The Tonight Show, 27
Tilden, Bill, 60

U.S. Open, 14, 20-21, 23-24, 26-27, 30-32, 34-35, 39-40, 42-46, 49, 54-56
U.S. Tennis Association, 18
United States Pro Indoors, 22

Volkov, Alexander, 44

Wilander, Mats, 21
Williams, Kimberley, 58-59
Wimbledon, 14, 22, 31, 38, 40-43, 45-47, 49, 54-55, 57-58, 60
Woodbridge, Todd, 58
World Team Cup, 40

Yzaga, Jaime, 49

DATE DUE			